Puppy Training

Housebreaking a Puppy in Record Time: The Ideal Beginner's Bundle

ANTHONY PORTOKALOGLOU

Disclaimer Notice

The techniques described in this book are for informational purposes only. All attempts have been made by the author to provide real and accurate content. No responsibility will be taken by the author for any damages cost by misuse of the content described in this book. Please consult a licensed professional before utilizing the information of this book.

I hope you will enjoy these books. I would be very grateful if you would consider leaving an honest review!

BOOKS IN THIS BUNDLE:

BOOK 1:

PUPPY TRAINING: HOW TO HOUSEBREAK YOUR PUPPY IN ONLY 7 DAYS"

BOOK 2:

PUPPY TRAINING: TRAIN YOUR PUPPY IN OBEDIENCE, POTTY TRAINING AND LEASH TRAINING IN RECORD TIME"

******BOOK 1******

PUPPY TRAINING

"HOW TO HOUSEBREAK YOUR PUPPY IN ONLY 7 DAYS"

ANTHONY PORTOKALOGLOU

Chapter 1: Understanding Your Puppy and the Pack Mentality

To train your puppy you first need to understand how your puppy assimilates his surroundings and where you will fit in his social structure. In canine's the pack mentality is very real, even when they are raised by humans.

First you must realize that in packs there is always an alpha. To your new puppy, you are simply a bigger dog. Your puppy has the intention of being the alpha, and your puppy will do whatever it wants, in the belief that it is alpha puppy until you show it otherwise. Being the "alpha" is not to you given it must be earned by you. There are dozens of videos on Facebook that are perfect illustrations of how disobedient, destructive and obstinate a pup can be when they have determined that they and not you are the alpha male.

In packs the leader is the alpha, he eats first, walks first, and controls the territory and will fight to maintain his leadership. This attitude is still entrenched in your puppy's DNA and your puppy is very much orientated to the idea it makes its own rules during those early months. Within that lovable diminutive ball of fluff is an unruly wolf pup waiting to defeat the leader and gain dominance of its territory. Pack leaders do not allow youngsters and lower pack members to have what they want when they want it. They use their authority to make them wait, sometimes denying them altogether. This sets a formidable example of who's in charge and teaches forbearance and self-control to high-strung, excitable young dogs. Making your dog sit and ignore things that excite him is a good way to establish your Leadership. It is also unwise to have your puppy sleep in bed with you. The alpha leader only allows his chosen female into his sleeping area. Any pack members failing to observe this strict rule do so at their peril. So, it's hardly unpredicted when owners allow their dogs into their bedroom that the puppies get the wrong idea. It is typical for a dog who occupies the owners sleeping quarters to assume that he is the alpha male and eventually can develop improper behavior. Oftentimes it is disobedience, more often it's possessiveness that can transform into aggression. Dogs are usually clever, maybe not as much as portrayed in television, but there is one area in which they are foolproof and that is reading other animals and that includes you!

Your dog will sense every slight change in your mood and react accordingly. If you are afraid he is going to misbehave he'll do exactly that. Pack Leaders control the pack by mental strength. You must convince him that you are that alpha male.

Your puppy will begin teething around two months of age and will want to bite and chew everything (including you). One technique to minimize this, is when your puppy gets his mouth on your hand quickly push your finger into his mouth until it reaches the gag reflex area. He will quickly lose interest in biting your hand to avoid that gag feeling. Remember to scold your puppy when you find him chewing something you don't want him to. A spank with a newly chewed shoe (item) will help your puppy know that he is not allowed to do that. Point and the chewed item and forcefully say "no". Once this is done, a light spank again will confirm the rebuke. Dogs have thicker skin than humans and the spank is not necessarily to inflict pain, but to show leadership. Remember your goal is to impose your will and become the alpha male. Do not punish your puppy after an incident has passed. They do not process information the same way, or reason the same way we do. To correct your puppy when time has passed in unfair and confusing to your puppy.

Play fighting is a good social skill for your puppy and will produce bonding between you as his master and establish your leadership level. It is important to show the puppy you are stronger than him and therefore the alpha. Holding your puppy down is an effective technique to establish dominance (not too firm and just a few seconds). Rolling the puppy over is another way of establishing your authority. Make sure you have toys for your puppy to play with and use them to play with him. Get a good variety, soft toys and hard toys to chew on, especially while he is teething. Tugging is a fun way to prove you are stronger and promote playfulness.

There are a variety of techniques to ensure that your puppy grows up to be an obedient, social and loving dog. It is also important to try and make sure your puppy associates with other dogs as they grow to help promote a pack mentality and good social skills. Also, in the early stages of your puppy be sure they have opportunity to interact with a variety of people to help them become social and friendly. It is a good idea to have your puppy interact with children as well. Children can be very intimidating to dogs and so for them to acclimate to them is very important. However, the most important thing is to make sure your puppy feels loved, by playing, petting, and treats. Puppies love human contact and affection. They are responsive both to a strong leader, but it is just as important to be a nurturing parent. It is essential to enjoy outdoor activities with your puppy whenever possible. When teaching your pet discipline, take a lesson from alpha wolves. Do not bark! Use the tone of your voice, your posture and uniformity to express your leadership. The wolves who are not an alpha but want to be alpha are the ones who mouth off. They have something to prove. You do not. You are already alpha and it is imperative that you act like one. Consistent treatment of your puppy lets him know what is expected of him. Prompt action against misbehavior shows him that you will not abide disobedience far better than all the yelling in the world. To control your puppy, you must first be in control of yourself! Self-control is the ability to control impulses and reactions, and is another name for self-discipline. Self-control, an aspect of inhibitory control, is the ability to regulate one's emotions, thoughts, and behavior in the face of temptations and impulses. As an executive function, self-control is a cognitive process that is necessary for regulating one's behavior in order to achieve specific goals.If you expect self-discipline from your puppy you must first learn to set the example. There will be many times in training your puppy that you will feel like your self-control is tested to its very limits. You will be tempted to wrongfully punish your pet when your life has been inconvenienced or your favorite things destroyed. Self-control is vital for overcoming obsessions, fears, addictions, and any kind of unsuitable behavior. It puts you in control of your life, your behavior, and your reactions. It strengthens your relationships, promotes patience and forbearance, and is an important tool in demonstrating you are the alpha male, and is the only tool to insure you are a fair and just pet owner.

By being aware and vigilant of your personal behavior, you will be able to be aware and vigilant of your dog's behavior. When you understand the pack mentality and give your little one confidence in your leadership they can love and respect you, and this will give you the position that you need to quickly and effectively housebreak your pet.

Chapter 2: Potty Training Basics – Getting it done in Seven Days!

Would you like to jump start the housebreaking process and have your puppy housebroken in seven days? Follow this schedule for seven straight days, and you will be well on your way to a puppy that understands exactly what is expected of him.

Adhere to 24-hour schedule. To house train your dog in 7 days, you need to meticulously follow a schedule. This will establish a routine for both you and your dog. Your puppy needs to go out first thing in the morning, after meals and play times, and before bedtime. Each moment should be accounted for. This is a sample routine for someone who is home all day.

7:00 a.m.: Time to wake up and take your puppy out to eliminate.

7:10-7:30 a.m.: Give your puppy some free time supervised by you.

7:30 a.m.: Give your puppy some food and some water.

8:00 a.m.: Take him to his designated potty spot.

8:15 a.m.: Give your puppy some free time supervised by you.

8:45 a.m.: Crate time

12:00 p.m.: Give your puppy some food and some water.

12:30 p.m.: Take him to his designated potty spot.

12:45 p.m.: Give your puppy some free time supervised by you.

1:15 p.m.: Crate time

5:00 p.m.: Give your puppy some food and some water.

5:30 p.m.: Take him to his designated potty spot.

6:15 p.m.: Crate time

8:00 p.m.: Water for an older puppy – food and water if under 4 months

8:15 p.m.: Take him to his designated potty spot.

8:30 p.m.: Give your puppy some free time supervised by you.

9:00 p.m.: Crate time

11:00 p.m.: Take him to his designated potty spot. Crate confinement overnight

During the night listen for whimpering and take your puppy outside to potty as necessary. The final chapter will cover the specifics of crate training in detail.

Like it or not, puppies need to eliminate. It can be exasperating for an owner, as puppies are not able to decipher the restrictions yet, which means elimination happens in places it should not. When puppies need to go, they go, and you must to be aware of that as an owner. This is basically the attitude that puppies take to everything, including eating, sleeping, and playing. They think of very little outside of those things. What that means is that the duty falls on you, the owner, to teach your puppy responsible behavior. You need to teach them what your requirements are, unless of course you just want them to keeping doing things the way you do not like.

Training your new puppy to potty at the right time and place can be one of the most challenging and yet important first steps for a long, happy life with each other. House soiling is a main reason dogs lose their homes or end up in shelters, as few people want to keep a dog who destroys their possessions and leaves a stinky mess to clean up.

There are three proven methods for training your puppy; frequent trips outdoors, paper training and crate training. Of course, there are positive and negative aspects of each, but they all can be prosperous if you adhere to a few basic ideas including:

- regulate your puppies diet
- have a consistent schedule for trips outside, feeding and exercise.
- provide consistent exercise
- praise your puppy for doing their business outside.

It is important to understand that the age of your puppy will determine his ability to wait to eliminate. The average measurement is one hour for each month of age. If you will pick up your puppy's water dish about two and a half hours before bedtime it will reduce the need for him to relieve himself during the night.

Chapter 3: Puppy Pads and Paper Training

In the traditional sense, paper or pad training is teaching your puppy to eliminate either on old newspapers or a pad placed in an area that is set aside as an indoor bathroom location for your puppy. Today there are options of specially made puppy pads as well as litter trays, and even fake grass boxes – but the method is still the same.

The concept is that a puppy gets used to relieving himself on paper and thus does not eliminate in places that they shouldn't. The paper absorbs and holds the urine and feces making it easier to clean up. For paper training, needed supplies include old newspapers (or pads), some food treats to reward eliminating in the right spot and some enzyme cleaning agents for the inevitable accidents. You will also possibly need an x-pen, play pen or baby gates depending on how you choose to confine your puppy to a single area when you must leave your home.

This method is one of the more difficult methods because you are offering two different options for your puppy. The ideal situation is that puppies learn to hold it indoors and only eliminate at a specific pre-ordained spot outdoors. Although this is the ideal scenario, it is not always possible due to a schedule that would make it impossible to get home several times a day. It would also be difficult for a tiny dog residing in a climate where there are brutal winters. Using the puppy pads will give your puppy the option of eliminating in an approved spot inside your home. As the dog matures, you can then work on having your dog eliminate outdoors all the time. The difficulty is that you are giving the puppy two options and at the beginning that can be just a bit confusing. But, if you stay consistent of placing the puppy regularly on the pad and giving a potty command using the same tone and same words each and every time. They will get the idea that that is the only location that is approved. But, because you will more than likely want the puppy to eliminate outdoors you will need to regularly take him out and using the same exact tone and exact same words as the indoor spot encourage him to potty in his outside designated potty spot.

This particular method relies mostly on three facts. First, puppies get accustomed to relieving themselves on the same surfaces or areas they have regularly been on previously. Secondly, puppies prefer to relieve themselves in areas where they can smell they have been before. Thirdly, puppies want to relieve themselves on softer, covered surfaces than on a cold, hard floor.

One way to do this is to paper a wide area, allow your puppy to potty there, slowly reduce the area that the papers cover then move the paper slowly to the spot you eventually want as a permanent toilet.

It is important to designate a place that is considered your puppies elimination area. Take your puppy to the same place each time. When choosing a room, opt for one with a hardwood, tiled or linoleum floor that's easily cleaned and will not soak up urine in case of accidents. It is best, if possible, to avoid carpeted areas as a puppy will prefer to relieve himself there with cushioning under his feet and not on the paper. A kitchen, bathroom or laundry room is usually ideal. An important tip would be to pick up the dirty paper as quickly as is possible. Do your best to clean it up as soon as it is dirtied. You want your puppy to be accustomed to a clean place and not even puppies want to spend time close to a large amount of their own feces and urine. However, when cleaning, keep a piece of the previously dirtied paper and use it to encourage eliminating in the spot you want. Just a small piece will be sufficient. Puppies like to eliminate where they've been previously. When they can smell a spot they've previously been, they are attracted to that spot to relieve themselves again. That is one reason why it is critical to avoid accidents, and why a thorough cleaning is necessary when there are accidents to avoid your puppy repeating that behavior.

Here are some techniques for proper cleanup for puppy accidents. With new accidents, pick up the solids and blot up as much liquid as possible. Do not use using ammonia-based cleaning products. Because urine has ammonia in it, those products may imitate the smell and make the area even more desirable as a spot for elimination. Once urine has dried on carpets or even walls it is even more difficult to discover exactly where the urine is located. If you will invest in a high quality black light you will be able to discover each and every accident site as the light will cause the urine to glow in the dark. Remember to check vertical areas such as walls and bedspreads that leg-lifting dogs like to target. To successfully clean urine you will not want a product that only covers up the area with perfumes, but one that will neutralize the foul-smelling urine. Urine is made of stick urea, urochrome (yellow color) and uric acid. The first two can be washed away, but uric acid is extremely difficult to break up and to remove from the surface. Successful products will not only clean away the urea and urochrome, but they will also neutralize the uric acid with enzymes or encapsulate the urine molecules that will contain the odor.

With paper training, you can use this in your favor by keeping some old soiled paper, and placing it in the area you would like your puppy to eliminate. It is best to put the designated potty area away from their bed and water. Carefully watch your puppy and if they try to eliminate in an area not covered by paper intercept and redirect them to the paper. Praise them when they successfully use the paper.

Any time they do eliminate on the paper by themselves, you also want to praise them heavily and offer some type of treat. This will help to more quickly encourage relieving themselves on the paper.

It is critical to make a schedule if you wish to have successfully housebreak your puppy. Your puppy has a tiny little bladder and liquid runs right through them. This is also true for food, it goes in and pretty much comes back out. It is very important to make sure you give your puppy many opportunities to eliminate outside and do the right thing. It is also helpful to know as it won't be very long at all after eating or drinking that you will need to take your puppy to his designated area.

Ten to twenty minutes after eating your puppy will be needed to be taken out.

As mentioned before, a good standard is that dogs can control their bladders for the number of hours corresponding to their age in months up to about nine months to a year. Be aware that that ten to twelve hours is a long time for anyone to hold it! A six-month-old puppy can rationally be required to hold it for about six hours. However, each puppy is an individual and the time factor will be different for each one. Size of the dog will also play a factor in how long they can hold it.

With very young puppies, you should expect to take the puppy out the very first thing in the morning and the very last thing at night. Just like a human baby, you will have to listen for whimpering and take your puppy to empty his bladder a few times a night especially if your puppy is under four months. He will need an opportunity to eliminate after playing, after waking from a nap, after chewing and playing with his toys, after eating and after drinking. In those very early days you could be taking your puppy out to his designated potty area a dozen times or more in a twenty-four-hour period. But, that diligence will pay off in huge dividends as your puppy will learn much more effectively and quickly what is expected of him regarding proper elimination. There are challenges that may have to be navigated. If you work you may need to make arrangements, be it taking your dog to work, hiring a dog walker, or enlisting the help of a friend or family member to ensure that early schedule is consistently adhered to. The sooner you convey the idea that there is an approved place to potty and places that are off limits, the more quickly you'll be able to put this messy chapter of your life behind you.

It is imperative to carefully evaluate your puppy and to discover his individual signals and indicators for the need to eliminate. Some puppies may be able to wait longer than others. Some puppies will have to go out each time they get excited or play hard. Some will lose control of their bladder if their owner expresses anger to them. Canine potty habits are certainly idiosyncratic, but all puppies, if evaluated, will give signals to express their intentions. Some signals might include whining, squatting, walking in circles, or sniffing around. When your very young puppy give you his indicator, pick him up right then and carry him to his designated potty spot. Do not expect him to walk to his potty spot, as he may not be able to make it.

Before deciding upon this method to housebreak your pet, we need to evaluate some of the disadvantages of this method in order for you to make a truly informed decision.

The main disadvantage of this technique is that you are training your puppy that it is okay to relieve himself inside your home. Now, if you plan to have a permanent indoor potty spot for your dog this is okay, but if your plans are to eventually have them relieve themselves outside this method as mentioned before can be confusing to your puppy. Because of this confusion, housebreaking generally takes a bit longer with this method and there are generally more accidents as well.

A second disadvantage of this method is that any papers accidently left lying around can be a target for elimination on by your puppy. If a newspaper is inadvertently left on the floor you may find some bad news inside!

A third disadvantage is that you will have more clean-up as the papers will need to be removed as quickly as possible for health and hygiene reasons. This method has the potential to leave your home smelling more like a kennel than a family dwelling.

A forth disadvantage is that some pets trained in this manner will use only paper and that will make training them to use the designated spot outside substantially more difficult.

This method of training is much more easily done in a practical sense with small dogs due to the sheer volume of waste that can be produced by a larger breed.

Chapter 4: The Diet of Your Puppy

Another extremely important factor is to control the diet. The digestive systems of puppies are immature and they are not able to handle a lot of food at one time. It is recommended that you break up the feedings into three or four small meals. Another very important factor is to give your puppy a high-quality food that is designed for puppies and has the greatest nutritional value and one that agrees with your puppy's digestion system.

Being aware of your puppy's stool is a very good way to determine if his diet is agreeable or not. If you are seeing consistent stools that are bulky, stinky or loose, you may want to discuss alternative food options with your vet. When a puppy is over-fed, it can cause diarrhea and that makes housetraining even more challenging. Also, especially during that very important first year, do not feed your puppy human food. It is truly best for your dog if human food is never a part of his diet.

One of the dangers of overfeeding is food bloat. Some breeds are more susceptible than others, but each owner needs to be aware. Puppies may be too young to figure out when their little tummies are full or may gobble their food too quickly. They may continue eating, or snacking, when they are not even hungry. Eating too much can cause food bloat. Over-eating can even cause a life-threatening condition called gastric dilation-volvulus. GDV simply means your puppy is in danger of suffering from a twisted stomach from overeating. The belly becomes distended and there can be unsuccessful retching and excessive salivating. It would be important to call your vet if you notice these symptoms as they can be life threatening.

Another danger of over-eating could be obesity. Your puppy is not able to understand how much food he needs, many times if there is food available he will eat it resulting in obesity. You do not want a chubby puppy that turns into a chubby adult dog as the negative health effects will shorten your dog's lifespan and possibly incur unwanted vet bills. The same maladies that plague overweight humans (diabetes, heart problems and hypothyroidism) tend to also plague overweight dogs. Healthy eating habits as a puppy usually translate to healthy habits in the adult dog.

A good diet will also help prevent skeletal problems. Puppy food is filled with a high amount of nutrients and the proper calories needed to build strong bones and teeth. Puppy formula will help your baby grow into a healthy adult. Too much food will accelerate his growth too quickly causing his little body to go into overdrive and create bone too quickly. A result would be the possibility of skeletal and joint problems as he ages. Some large breeds are especially susceptible. Similar problems can result from feeding puppy food to your adult dog.

We want to get it just right and since a puppy's eyes are bigger than his stomach he may feel he needs more food than he does. Because of his stomach being so small, he will need to eat many small meals as opposed to one or two big ones. Four meals a day until around four months old is a good rule of thumb. Then you can try lowering it to three slightly larger meals. By around six months of age you should be able to feed him twice daily. Study your breed to know the benefits and pitfalls. If you have a mixed breed then concentrate on his dominate breed and do your best to accommodate his needs. Some smaller breeds will mature faster some as early as ten months of age. While other larger breeds may take up to a couple of years to mature. Your vet is a good place to gather the needed information for your particular dog breed.

Another thing to be work on with your puppy is the fact you do not want him aggressive over his food. From the time he is very small, periodically take away his food as he begins eating and return it shortly after. Another thing to do is to place your hand into his dish while he is eating and take food out or move his food around with your hand. Your puppy needs to understand that you have full authority of his food area. Puppies that are allowed to eat without any distractions or challenges can become very aggressive and attack anyone who dares to enter the sacred area of their food bowl. To prevent this from happening make sure that you do this often during the first six months and periodically afterwards as a refresher course. The same is true with rawhides and such, your puppy needs to know that you can take away his food and toys anytime you please. Since you give it back shortly he will begin to understand he will not go hungry, and these actions will give you freedom to be in his food area. If possible when he is young have people that are not in your household to do the same procedures with him. It could save an attack over him protecting his food bowl in the future.

Chapter 5: The Importance of Praise

The importance of praising your puppy cannot be over emphasized. There are times when a puppy will need to be scolded or corrected; but if you scold or punish a puppy after he has soiled your rug or floor he will not understand what you are doing and it will only confuse and alienate him. And to be honest, that soiling was your fault. You did not watch for his indicators that he was in need to go out and potty. You will need both positive and negative reinforcements to train your puppy, but you must be fair and just with your puppy. You wouldn't spank a baby for pooping in his diaper and neither is it just to discipline a puppy who is still trying to figure out this business of where and when he can and can't go potty. Go over the top with praise and excitement when your puppy goes outside. Give a little treat, cheer, clap, cuddle whatever it takes to let that little one to understand that he did great! Be effusive in letting him know that nothing is more important than him going potty in his designated place!

It is wise to keep your puppy in a contained area that has no rugs if possible during the training process. If you missed the cues, or no one was available to take him out – just clean it up and promise yourself that YOU will do better next time. It would be wise to invest in a cleaner that will kill odors and help remove the scent so he is not tempted by the smell to use that spot again. It is vital that you read labels very carefully and make sure that the cleaner is not toxic to your little one! If your puppy urinates on your carpet, blot of as much of the liquid as is possible before applying cleaners.

Since prevention is the key thing, if you catch the dog starting to squat pick him up and rush outside. If he does his business then praise, praise, praise! If you are trying to show him the pad is his alternative indoor spot you could carry him there.

When it comes to housetraining, prevention is the key factor that will enable you to be quickly successful in this endeavor.

A dog's size is also going to be a factor in potty training. "Toy" dogs can be trained with diligence, but it will take a great deal of consistency and perhaps a bit more time. If your little dog is going to spend many hours without the opportunity to eliminate some trainers recommend teaching little dogs to use potty boxes designed for indoor use or even the puppy pads. This is a concept much like a kitty litter box for cats.

If your puppy keeps eliminating indoors in the same spot where he has had an accident it is probably because you didn't clean up the urine effectively and there is residual odor remaining.

A common mistake is giving your dog the run of the house before they are truly ready. A pet owner feels like their puppy has the idea or has behaved well and declare victory too soon. Then they are angry when they come to a destroyed piece of furniture or mess on the floor. There are times when the owner is away and either the puppy gets excited, fearful or most common just plain ole bored. The pet owner comes back to a mess and the puppy has no understanding of why he is in so much trouble and why his owner is angry with him.

Chapter 6: Understanding a Urinary Tract Infection

If your puppy has gone an extensive time with success and then out of the blue begins to urinate indoors one of the first things to do is to make sure that are no physical issues promoting this behavior. A urinary tract infection or bladder infection can many times cause your pet to have issues with elimination.

Here are some tips to determine if your puppy or dog has a urinary tract infection and what to do about it. If you puppy is needing more trips outside it is because a urinary tract infection gives an increased urge to urinate usually resulting in more whining, barking and trips to the yard. You may also find yourself needing to refill their water bowl more often, as dogs with UTIs are generally thirstier – this also accounts for the increase in urination. Sometimes a dog with a UTI will need to go so often they stop trying to go to their designated outside location, or pad. Because the urge to urinate is sudden and uncontrollable it will result in a regression in this area of potty training. Another symptom of a serious UTI would be blood. Blood in your dog's urine is never a good sign, and this symptom can be especially tricky to detect – unless, of course, the urine is on your favorite white carpet. Blood oftentimes looks brown and not red, so be aware. A round of antibiotics from your vet can have your puppy feeling better in just a few days.

Chapter 7: Training Without a Crate and Without Puppy Pads

There are people who just do not like the idea of putting their puppy in a crate, or even have adopted a puppy that was abused and a crate was involved, or even the fact that they may just not have room for a crate. Regardless of the reason, the good news is that you can succeed at house training without a crate if you can devote 100% of your time to this endeavor.

The only way to successfully housebreak your puppy is to give the puppy constant supervision. This particular method is best suited to people who can spend all day with their puppy. People that work from home, or the retired. It's also a preferred method for people who just do not agree with the use of a crate, or have a crate phobic puppy or dog.

What Is 'Constant Supervision' House Training?

We will cover a range of procedures that do not involve the use of a crate. This method will rely on constantly watching your dog or puppy.

Using a crate takes of advantage of the fact a puppy will not potty inside their den if it isn't roomy enough that they can toilet at one end and sleep at the other. In crate method an unsupervised puppy is placed into a crate. However, if you are not using a crate, no other confined space will be small enough that your puppy is deterred from eliminating in there.

If you choose to train your puppy without a crate you have no opportunity to take your eyes off of your puppy and still be guaranteed that they won't soil your carpet. Each mistake is a missed teaching time to train to do the right thing. This results in a backward step in training as well as cleaning up the mess that your puppy made.

So, the only fast tract to success is constant, and this does mean constant, supervision. You must be diligent to watch him to make sure he does not eliminate on your floors and carpet; which means he cannot be left unsupervised.

Therefore, the only quick path to success is constant, and I mean CONSTANT supervision. You must watch them like a hawk to be sure he won't potty on your floors and carpets. He can never be left unsupervised.

This method means a puppy that is not housebroken can never be left alone or unwatched in the home. A puppy can relieve himself where he shouldn't in a matter of a few seconds, and to train your puppy properly this must be prevented. You will need to be aware of your puppies indicators that he is about to relieve himself and be ready to take them to their designated potty location. Each puppy will have their own unique indicator, but generally it will be sniffing the ground, whining, attempting to get to a quiet location, circling or even squatting. The pet owner will need to be aware of their puppies behavior at all times to prevent accidents or immediately correct them by getting them immediately to the proper spot with a firm "No!" for the action.

You may be thinking that this sounds like a LOT of work and truly it is, but there are ways to make this training method a bit easier.

Most often when a puppy is sitting in your lap or sleeping near you they will not eliminate on you, so that would give an opportunity for a bit of relaxation of your guard. When you are going to be in different rooms you could attach them to the leash and keep them with you, which will help you realize when they need to go and also prevent them from sneaking off to relieve themselves. In this method of training it is imperative that you either are watching them or that there is a physical connection to know exactly what they are doing at all times.

Also, the use of this method of training requires extreme diligence; it is the method that requires the least equipment. With this method, you will not need puppy pads, crates or play pens. You will need a collar, leash, food treats and enzyme cleaners for the occasional accident. It is unreasonable to assume that during this training time you will never leave your puppy, so you may need a sectioned off area (preferable puppy proofed), use a baby gate or some type of way to contain your puppy when you do have to leave, along with pads for the inevitable accident. It would be wise to have a location that is easily cleaned.

Ways to create a sanctioned area would be to use a baby gate or pet barrier to limit your puppy to a single room, usually one with no carpet. You can also purchase a puppy "x-pen" which effectively fences off a small section to keep your puppy contained to that particular location. These spaces must be large enough for bedding, water at one end and newspaper or puppy pads at the other.

To be fair, training without a crate is the most difficult method as trying to constantly supervise anything is challenging. Even those who work from home or are retired have cooking, cleaning, laundry, calls, chores and more. By comparison, accidents will be more likely without a temporarily space to confine your puppy during the time they are supposed to be holding their bladder. Since you are not giving an alternative indoor potty area such in paper or pad training, you will always have to be on high alert for those indicators that your puppy needs to go. If you have the time and are always home, this method is effective and you are sure to succeed.

Regardless of the method of choice for you, any puppy needs to be closely supervised and interrupted when they are ready to eliminate in a spot that is not their designated potty area.

Chapter 8: Crate training

Crate training is the most effective, fool proof and humane method to train your puppy, especially if your goal is to train your puppy in seven days! Some believe crate training a dog to be cruel or barbaric. However, if you will evaluate crate training from a dog's viewpoint, you will find that it actually meets an innate desire for a safe place to call his own. Dogs are basically what we call den animals. It is in their genetic makeup to want a secure and sheltered area to rest. Many times in the effort to create their own "den" a puppy or dog will curl up in a box or under a low table. Crate training can help to satisfy this very natural instinct in your puppy, and will provide you with several benefits as well. Offering your dog its own crate meets your pet's instinctive needs and allows you some control in housebreaking endeavors.

So understanding what makes a good crate for your puppy would be your first step. The most effective crate is one that is just barely big enough so that your dog can lie, stand and turn around. If you give the puppy too much space it will destroy the den concept, and will give your pet the option of soiling half of the crate and still having a clean area in which to rest.

There are a variety of materials and brands to choose from. The next decision will be whether plastic or wire will work best for your puppy's needs. Crates that are made from molded plastic are easy to clean, draft-free and because of the limited visibility are more like dens. Depending on your dogs size and type of coat and what conveniences you will need in a crate, plastic may be what you are looking to use. Some advantages to a plastic crate are that they provide better insulation for your puppy.

If you own a puppy, small dog, or dog with a short coat, then plastic crates can help him to retain more of his body heat. This can be helpful in cold or wet climates. This may be a disadvantage if you live in a warmer climate or have a long haired dog. Another benefit to a plastic crate is the fact that it offers more privacy. With generally fewer openings for the dog to see out it will give a feeling of a safe den-like space. The fact that the puppy's view is blocked will eliminate some things that might distract him and cause him to whine and cry. If travel is in your foreseeable future, a plastic crate can be airline approved, whereas a wire crate cannot. If travel is in the foreseeable future for you and your puppy, first check with your airlines to make sure the plastic dog crate of your choice would meet their safety guidelines. There are several types of plastic dog crates that come apart for storage. Some crates are designed for the top to be removable so that the bottom can be used as a dog bed. Not every crate has these versatile features, so read carefully what your crate is capable of doing before purchasing. Generally, even a bigger plastic dog crate can be very light, which is something to consider if you will be moving the crate often.

Although there are many positive features, the plastic crate does have downsides. In a plastic crate there is a decreased amount of ventilation and air movement. So the crate has to potential to become very stuffy for your pet. Another disadvantage is that your pet may feel too isolated. If your puppy is very people oriented or has become very attached to you, the plastic crate may make him feel isolated and separated from you. Storage can take more room as a plastic crate cannot fold flat and will not breakdown to the degree that a wire or soft sided type will. The biggest disadvantage to a plastic crate is that plastic is porous and the odors can become imbedded in the material of the crate itself. This makes it more difficult to keep the crate clean.

Many dog owners prefer a wire dog crate as they have the great advantage of providing excellent ventilation. Because of their wire mesh panels they are also the best selection for dogs that have chewing habits since it is impossible for them to chew through stainless steel or galvanized wire. Another advantage of wire crates is they are completely collapsible which enables easy storage and ease when they must be transported from one location to another. A number of brands come with a divider panel; this will be extremely helpful as your puppy increases size. Some brands feature a two door system with one door on the front and one door on the backside of the crate. In these particular crates the doors are usually secured by wire mesh hooks or by a drop pin. Wire crates are generally made from powder coated or galvanized steel or stainless steel. One of the main highlights in the "pro" category for the wire crate is that there is normally a plastic pan at the bottom which will slide in and out for easy cleaning. The excellent ventilation also makes for a reduction of trapped odors.

Wire dog crates come in a variety of sizes and most offer divider panels. If getting a large breed puppy, you can buy a larger crate than he's needs so he can still use it when he reaches his adult size. Considering a crate can be one of the more expensive items you'll buy for your dog, this can save you money in the long run. A divider can be used to keep two dogs separated without getting a second kennel, or can be helpful if you have a puppy that will grow to be a large size dog. It will save you money by only having to buy one crate that will last your puppies growing spurt. When a small puppy is in a large crate the "den like" experience is lost, a divider wall can give that secure closed in feeling. This problem is overcome with a divider panel that can be adjusted as your puppy grows.

Your puppy may grow to enjoy the run of the house, but sometimes he needs to be put in his crate. A wire general cage dog crate allows your dog to feel more like a part of what is going on in your home because he can see what is going on around him. Wire crates provide a better view if car traveling is something that is frequently done.

Nothing is perfect and a wire crate is not an exception. A disadvantage is that even when there are perfectly assembled they can have a loose feel about them. In time the doors can lose their alignment making the locking feature harder to use. Also a very large wire crate can be bulky and heavy making it awkward or difficult to move. Because a wire crate offers great ventilation it may need to be covered to keep out drafts and to make it appear more den-like.

Once a crate has been purchased, you will want to give your puppy or dog time to investigate. Just leave the crate on the floor with the door open until your puppy becomes used to having it around. Placing dog treats and a towel might help your puppy gain an interest in exploring the crate. After your puppy is familiar with the crate, close your dog inside the crate for ten to fifteen minutes. Stay right there with your puppy perhaps even putting your fingers through the wire of the crate. Your puppy needs to be assured that this new environment is safe and secure. After ten or fifteen minutes open the door and let the puppy stay or leave at his will. This should be done several times that first day getting your little one accustomed to his crate. The crate is to be his safe space and should never be used to punish your puppy. The time in the crate should be as enjoyable as is possible. Toys and treats can help to establish this setting of harmony and peace.

Crate training helps you teach your little one not to use the bathroom inside. Dogs instinctively desire to keep their den clean. Dogs do not want to sleep in a soiled area and will do all within their power to hold it until they are taken to their designated potty spot. If you have a crate that is the proper fit for your puppy he is going to do all in his power to refrain from using the bathroom until you let him outside. Crate training makes it a simple way to schedule regular trips to his designated potty spot.

It is important to determine the crate's ideal location. You need to put the crate in a location that will remain consistent. This may be a high-traffic area where your family spends a lot of time, but you may also want to provide the dog with some rest time removed from activity, especially at night. Dogs are social animals and some breed even more so than others. They enjoy being near their family so that they can see what is going on around them and can feel like a part of things. This is very fulfilling to a dog. Since being in a crate should be a positive experience and they should want to spend time there, you don't want to stick them away in a quiet room or out of the way place in the house. They will feel punished, excluded and isolated; and that will not make for a serine, happy puppy. Make sure you place the crate in a busy area of the home where they are able to see and hear what is going on with their family. Usually kitchen or living room areas are ideal locations for a crate. Keep in mind that you would like this area to be free of uncomfortable drafts, not too close to a heat source (radiator, fireplace or vent). You will want to avoid direct sunlight. As much as you are able to give the location of your crate should be neither too hot nor too cold.

If your puppy is very young, you may want to consider moving the crate into your bedroom at night, or placing them in a portable carrier or second crate. The very young puppy has just gone from being with his mother and perhaps siblings to being alone. This can leave them stressed and feeling abandoned which will result in whining and crying. You don't want to make the mistake of putting the puppy in bed with you as that will confuse him as to who is the alpha – him or you. But, neither do you want him to feel frightened and alone.

A puppy will get great comfort and a feeling of safety and security being able to sleep near their family, especially during those first few days in a strange new place.

It isn't essential you have them sleep in your bedroom with you, but it may be beneficial. After a few days, begin to move the crate slowly to where you want them to sleep as they have time to adjust to their new environment. Simply move the crate further away every few nights until you have removed them from the bedroom and where you want them to be.

Some ideas of the proper toys and bedding to place in your crate would be tough chew toys. There are many benefits to leaving two or three tough chew toys in the crate with your puppy. It will provide your puppy with something to occupy their minds and keep them from becoming bored. It will give them an alternative to chewing up their bedding, which could be detrimental to their health. It reinforces that being in the crate is a time for some of their favorite things, thus making the crate a happy place for them. It also will help reduce the likelihood of your puppy chewing on your belongings.

It is important to be aware that soft stuffed teddy bears and easily chewed squeaky toys should only be given to your puppy under supervision and never left in the crate. They will likely get destroyed, but your puppy could inject pieces causing intestinal blockages.

The most important thing about crate training is to follow a strict schedule so that your puppy becomes accustomed to routine! If this sample schedule is adhered to you will be well on your way to having your puppy potty trained in record time!

Adhere to a 24-hour schedule. To house train your dog in 7 days, you need to meticulously follow a schedule. This will establish a routine for both you and your dog. Your puppy needs to go out first thing in the morning, after meals and play times, and before bedtime. Each moment should be accounted for. This is a sample routine for someone who is home all day.

7:00 a.m.: Time to wake up and take your puppy out to eliminate.

7:10-7:30 a.m.: Give your puppy some free time supervised by you.

7:30 a.m.: Give your puppy some food and some water.

8:00 a.m.: Take him to his designated potty spot.

8:15 a.m.: Give your puppy some free time supervised by you.

8:45 a.m.: Crate time

12:00 p.m.: Give your puppy some food and some water.

12:30 p.m.: Take him to his designated potty spot.

12:45 p.m.: Give your puppy some free time supervised by you.

1:15 p.m.: Crate time

5:00 p.m.: Give your puppy some food and some water.

5:30 p.m.: Take him to his designated potty spot.

6:15 p.m.: Crate time

8:00 p.m.: Water for an older puppy – food and water if under 4 months

8:15 p.m.: Take him to his designated potty spot.

8:30 p.m.: Give your puppy some free time supervised by you.

9:00 p.m.: Crate time

11:00 p.m.: Take him to his designated potty spot. Crate confinement overnight

Make sure to give your puppy a bathroom break during the night. The maximum time you are able to leave a young puppy is four hours so with a very young puppy you will need to set your alarm clock for every two to three hours. After the alarm goes off take your puppy out of the crate and give him a chance to relieve himself in his designated potty spot. Then quietly put him back into the crate. Older dogs can wait longer, but you need to make sure they do not go in their crate overnight, or all that hard work in the day time is basically undone. During this time do not fuss or even speak to the puppy except to give him his potty instructions – the same words and same tone as during the day. You don't want to give him the idea that night-time is play time.

A crate is an ideal place to keep your belongings safe and secure and your puppy safe and secure while you are away. Another thought is that a crate is also the most secure and convenient way to transport your dog as it will keep him protected while in the car and is a necessity for airline travel.

As with anything, a crate can be abused. You may be tempted to keep your puppy there throughout the day or to use it as a way to punish him. This will just undermine the training process and perhaps make your puppy hate the crate when it should in fact be his haven!

When you are crate training all feedings initially should be done inside of the crate. Make sure you leave the door open while you are feeding your puppy. The association with food will make it a great place for him.

Your puppy needs you as the owner to be consistent in your routine but also in the words you use to instruct him. Just as you will want to use the same phrase with the same exact inflection when teaching your puppy his designated potty spot; you will also want to use the same phrase and same inflection when instructing him to get inside of his crate. You need to choose the same word each time. A command such as "crate time" or "get in your Kennel" with the same exact hand gesture will help him to understand what is expected of him. When the puppy goes in say the command, and when you feed him at meal times say the same command. When your puppy obeys give him a treat to show him your pleasure. It is best that your puppy not associate his crate with being alone. So in the early days of training make sure that you or someone familiar is able to be with him as he acclimates to his crate. Those early days can also be benefited by keeping a puppy journal. It may sound impractical to keep a journal of the times your puppy needs to go potty, but it may in fact prevent unwanted accidents to have a written documentation of his successes and his accidents. A regular feeding schedule will help to insure a more regular bathroom schedule. Remember it is critical to not punish your puppy for accidents, teaching your puppy to eliminate outdoors is a process that takes patience and time.

Chapter 9: Conclusion

Being a pet owner is one of the most fulfilling roles available to mankind. The love and adoration so freely given can be so gratifying. The soothing sensation of running your hands down their fur and looking into deep loving eyes can make the coldest heart melt. That exuberance and devotion that is lavished completely on you just for showing up can make your feel like a million dollars! If you want to be needed and to be loved, a dog is usually hands down the best choice of all.

However, with that love, acceptance and devotions comes responsibility and commitment! I think we have all seen the videos and clips of dogs with their bones showing through their skin, whimpering in the cold; unloved, uncared for and neglected. We all wonder to ourselves – how could anyone do something so dastardly? I can't imagine anyone starting out to neglect and harm their pet, but yet we have seen that scenario take place. Dog ownership is not something to be entered into frivolously. Owning a dog is a long-term emotional and financial obligation. Before deciding that a certain dog is right for you, you must make an honest assessment as to whether your home is right for any dog.

Before getting a puppy you need to ask yourself a few questions:

- Do I have the finances to own a dog?
- Is my space adequate for a dog?
- Is my schedule adaptable to having a dog?
- Am I willing to commit to training my dog?
- Can I control my emotions when angry or frustrated?

If you answered yes to the above questions, then you are ready to enjoy the pleasures and enjoyment of being a dog owner! You and your family members should decide who will be responsible for food, water, walking, exercise, clean-up and grooming. Post a schedule of tasks in a visible area of the house to remind everyone of their responsibilities.

It is always a wise idea to Dog-Proof Your Home! Prepare your home before your new dog arrives. Move breakables or "chewables" to higher ground. Make electrical cords inaccessible to inquisitive paws and noses. Block off any area of the house that you want off-limits. Put the lid down on your toilet and your shoes up in your closet. Block off access or put away plants that may be toxic to dogs.

And last but not least, enjoy your new puppy and make many happy memories that you will cherish for a lifetime!

*****BOOK 2*****
PUPPY TRAINING

"TRAIN YOUR PUPPY IN OBEDIENCE, POTTY TRAINING AND LEASH TRAINING IN RECORD TIME"

ANTHONY PORTOKALOGLOU

Contents

CHAPTER 1: WELCOMING YOUR NEW PUPPY

Dog is the most popular pet that individuals seek for. They have been domesticated for more than 14 thousand years which is longer than any other animal. Dogs make it their mission to make their humans happy, however there are important facts and considerations encompassed in it. You must realize that molding a puppy into a balanced canine companion requires a considerable investment of time and energy.

Puppy training starts the moment you bring your puppy home. Whatever he does, you must react properly or he will learn the wrong things.

Once you have made the positive decision of getting a puppy, you need to choose the most appropriate breed, taking into consideration many factors including your lifestyle, home, surroundings, work pattern, family, other pets, budget, etc. Look in books and on the internet to find out about the different breeds and their specific needs. Talk to your vet, friends, family and neighbors who own dog breeds you are considering. Having narrowed your selection, you need to look for suitable breeders. Once you've made a shortlist, it's a good idea to meet the breeders and their puppies.

THE RIGHT BREED FOR YOU

Choosing to bring a puppy home is a big decision – a commitment of up to 15 years or more. Look ahead – your cute new puppy will soon be a fully-grown dog requiring years of affection, nourishment, care, and training. If you are planning to get a pet for you or your kids, learn how to choose a puppy through the given details below. Make it as your guide to ensure that you will not regret in the end and you will be happy with your pet. Selecting the right puppy involves a personal decision relying on the following factors: lifestyle temperature and budget of the family. Your dog must be compatible and comfortable with your family to achieve mutual benefits.

1. Lifestyle – Dogs enjoy outdoors and physical activities. Your family should be capable of providing the kind of activity for them. If

your children love outdoor activities and sports, they will certainly love being with active dogs, such as Dalmatians or Golden Retrievers. If not, there are also other breeds of dogs that can meet the same temperament.

2. Price – The price of a dog depends on its breed. As a family, it is crucial to determine the amount that you can spend to your dog each month. Calculate the amount of your dog's foods, healthcare and grooming to determine the total amount you need to save.

3. Temperament – Gregarious and outdoing kids have a better relationship with dogs that are more approachable and friendlier. Certainly your family needs to meet the needs of your dog.

4. Care and Grooming – Your dog also need proper grooming and care regularly. You should also know that some breeds require more care grooming than others. A dog that has curly or long coats should be groomed for many times within a week. It is advised that you stick to a breed of dog that has shorter coats and needs less maintenance especially if it is your kids who will take care of that dog.

5. Living Situation – The kind of dog that you are going to select should also depend on the kind of living situation you have. Larger breeds are perfect for families that have their own home and got enough space for exercise and play time. Another thing to consider is the climate since there are dogs that survive in a warmer or colder weather.

You may also include the size of the dog in the list. Remember that small dogs have been very vulnerable and delicate. If you accidentally stepped on them or mishandled them, this can lead to serious injury. They are also more sensitive to cold temperatures, thus, keep them warm especially during the winter.

By learning how to choose a dog, you can easily find the perfect breed of dog for you and your family. Reflect on the kind of lifestyle you and your family can manage with the kind of dog being taken care of.

SELECTING A BREEDER

The breeder you go with has a huge influence on the wellbeing of your future puppy, so be prepared to ask some questions that will help you make the best choice. If possible, ask for references from other owners. This is a crucial decision and must be taken seriously. You must take into consideration the following:

• Follow recommended breeding guidelines

• Make use of health screening schemes, such as testing for hip problems and eye conditions, which will help owners to predict the future health of their puppy.

• Ensure the puppy is seen with its mother, to give an indication of how the puppy is likely to turn out.

• Be prepared to answer your questions about the breed.

• Be there as a point of contact throughout the puppy's life to ensure that the dog and owner have a happy and fulfilling relationship. If a breeder doesn't follow these guidelines and if the puppies do not appear happy and are not kept in good conditions, then look elsewhere.

• Assessing the breeder and their puppies. Are both parents healthy? Does the breeder have any relevant health test results for the sire and dam? This is very important – particularly if there are any health risks associated with the breed, e.g. hip dysplasia. If you are unsure, take the registration numbers and you can check for yourself the health tests and pedigrees.

SOCIALIZING YOUR PUPPY

Socialization is extremely important to prevent bad behavior problems such as anxiety, fear, shyness and aggression later on life. Socialization period starts around 3 weeks of age and closes between 16-20 weeks. The key is to make sure your puppy gets exposed to everything he may ever be exposed to during his lifetime, while he is very young. Exposing your new puppy to pleasant experiences such as strangers, children and other dogs, is critical to having a well-balanced adult dog.

Follow the below steps to give your puppy the best start possible. Try to expose your dog regularly to all of the things and situations you would like him to be able to cope with calmly in the future. Progress slowly enough so that it is easy for your dog to enjoy the sessions. It will seem like a lot of time to spend at first, but it will pay off with a well-behaved dog! Below are some examples:

• Meeting new people of all types, including children, men, crowds, people wearing hats, etc.

• Meeting new dogs (due to disease risk, do not bring your pup to areas with lots of dogs until after 4 months– unless it's a well-run puppy kindergarten). Positive training classes are great for this purpose.

• Exposure to other pets such as cats, horses, birds.

• Riding in the car (be sure to restrain him using a secured crate or dog seatbelt for safety).

• Being held, touched all over and in different ways, being bathed and groomed.

• Visiting the veterinarian's office, groomer, daycare, boarding kennel.

• Exposure to loud noises and strange objects (ex. umbrella opening).

•Exposure to traffic, motorcycles, bicycles, skateboards, joggers.

• Getting him used to being left alone for a few hours at a time.

CHAPTER 2: PUPPY HEALTH CARE

Puppy healthcare isn't 'rocket science' but sometimes it can be tricky to identify when your puppy is really sick as well as what type of preventative care is needed, or what to do about common health issues.

1. Find a good vet

Some canine diseases are very serious and can be fatal even with treatment. Highly effective vaccinations are available to help prevent some of these diseases. At 8 weeks of age, puppies should receive their first vaccination; this is temporary and needs to be followed up with another one at 12 weeks. After the 12 week vaccination, you can then take your puppy out in public areas. Your puppy will need annual boosters.

More than 85% of dogs over four years old will experience some form of gum disease which can lead to irreversible damage to the teeth and to other organs in the body. Prevention is possible with a well balanced diet including raw bones (or specifically formulated dental bones) on a weekly basis, regular dental check-ups at least yearly and teeth brushing.

Do not give unprescribed medications to your dog without checking with a vet first. Even aspirin and paracetamol can be dangerous if given incorrectly, especially if your pet is on medication or has a medical condition.

2. Shop quality food

Puppies grow fast that's why providing the proper nutrition is important for building strong teeth and bones as well as adding muscle.

Puppies should get solid food starting at about four weeks. Ask your vet which puppy food he or she recommends, how often to feed, and what portion size to give your puppy. There are dozens of varieties of puppy food, however choose among the best quality and the one that will meet your pup's nutritional requirements.

3. Early Signs of Illness

Here are eight common signs to watch for your puppy. Make sure to contact your vet for advice.

1. Vomiting
2. Weight loss
3. Lack of appetite
4. Diarrhea
5. Difficulty breathing
6. Pale gums
7. Red eyes or eye discharge
8. Coughing

CHAPTER 3: THE SCIENCE OF TREATS

To train your puppy, whether lure and reward training, or clicker training, treats are a brilliantly useful reinforcement tool to use during training. Training using treats is easy and fun for both dog and human. Puppies can learn new behaviors quite quickly with this kind of training.

Always when teaching a new command, you need to reward your dog every time that he does what you ask correctly. Once he comfortable executing the command, it's a good idea to change the way you reward by giving the reward every now and then. This way your dog will try 'harder' for his reward. Always verbally praise your dog each time, even if he is not being rewarded with a treat.

Treats need to be pea-sized and easy to get to (in your pocket, training pouch or a nearby table top)

Distracting environments call for better treats. You can usually get away with something like Cheerios in the house without much going on, but for outside leash walking practice, whip out the cubed cheddar or dried liver. A mix of treats is ideal so that the puppy never knows what's next.

TREAT IDEAS:

• Pre-cooked, frozen chicken breast: Toss it in the fridge to thaw the day before class. Cut into small pieces.

• Cubed lunch meat (to dry it out a bit: microwave it 3 times for 30 seconds sandwiched between pieces of paper towel).

• Shredded cheese

• Cream cheese, peanut butter or Easy Cheese (a lick per behavior! Also great for grooming practice and stuffing in Kong when your dog will be alone for a while).

• Kibble (dry food) – Try placing some in a paper bag with a couple of pieces of bacon to stinkify" it.

• Dried liver

• Beef Jerky

- Imitation crab (try peeling the layers apart and placing them in a frost-free freezer in a colander to dry them out)
- Meat baby food.
- Commercial dog treats (be sure to check the ingredients for nasties such as artificial colors, preservatives, and by-products.

CHAPTER 4: HOW TO INTRODUCE YOUR PUPPY TO OLDER DOGS

Many puppy owners believe that getting a new puppy to the family will be pleasant experience, however many times they are disappointed when that doesn't happen. In order to make the process of introducing a new puppy to your current dog as pleasant as possible is good to know in advance what to expect.

Puppies have a different play style than older dogs. They don't follow the rules of adult dogs. Adult dogs have a certain way to greet each other or a way to invite play or to stop it. Actually puppies don't even know that rules exist. They usually play too rough using their mouth.

Your adult dog will be a valuable teacher to your new puppy as long as his behavior is appropriate, meaning that he is not 'connecting' with the puppy. He will first teach the puppy where the lines are drawn. Moreover he will teach him to stop jumping on the head or biting ears and tails or barking in the face or even come any closer is not allowed.

Before meeting:

Make sure that both the puppy and adult dog are up to date with their vaccinations and they have been given their medication for worms and parasites. Since the adult dog will most probably not share anything with your new puppy, it is a wise precaution to buy a new set of feeding bowls, toys and a bed.

First meeting:

It is advisable to set up the first meeting between the puppy and the adult dog, in a neutral area such us a park or the street in front of your house. Allow them to greet and sniff each other while they are on their leashes. Keep their leaches loose and try to stay as relaxed as possible as dogs can pick up any tense feelings.

Most likely your new puppy will display submissive behavior such as lying down and rolling over. At this stage your adult dog might growl which is totally normal behavior from a socialized dog. It is his way of teaching the puppy some 'manners'. Your adult dog may choose to play or ignore the puppy. The body language of an invitation to play is dog's front legs goes down and the tail goes up.

Keep the initial meeting short. As soon as you arrive home let your adult dog's off leash but keep the puppy on his leash and let them walk around the room. If your adult dog shows friendly manners, then let off the puppy's leash as well and keep supervising the two dogs. It is advisable to continue close supervision for a couple of weeks. Watch for situations which may trigger aggression. Keep your daily routines as normal and make the puppy to fit into the activities such as walk, play and meal time.

Additionally, try to spent time alone with each dog separately, so that your puppy gets the chance to develop a bond with you and in the same time your adult dog to continue receiving the attention he used to. Lastly feed your dogs separately from their own feeding bowls and discourage to bully each other during meal time. In case they start a fight then stop it as soon as possible in order not to develop an aggressive behavior. With time and effort, the puppy and the adult dog will learn to accept each other.

CHAPTER 5: SEPARATION ANXIETY

Separation anxiety is when your puppy exhibits stress and/or behavioral problems when he is left alone. This is the number one reason why owners get rid of their puppies. Fortunately, separation anxiety can be treated by implementing some simple steps.

The following is a list of signs that may indicate separation anxiety:

• puppy seems to worry
• destroys stuff
• follows you from room to another
• excessive barking or howling.
• chewing furniture and frantic scratching at doors or windows
• attempts to escape from the room or crate
• he follows you around closely

These are some basic things you can do to help ease separation anxiety:

Exercise

You need to make sure that your puppy gets plenty of physical exercise especially when you own a high energy breed. However you should not over-exercise your puppy. Tiring him out will make him more content to sleep or just take it easy when left alone.

Crate Training

If you train your dog to be content in a crate your puppy will feel safer and more comfortable in his crate when left alone. Puppies that have been properly introduced to their crate prefer the safety of a crate to being left alone in a big open house.

Leaving your dog alone

Leave your puppy alone in a room for 5 minutes. Then extend the time to 15 minutes and then to 1 hour. Try this exercise several times a day and continue to increase the time you spend away until you can leave your puppy alone for more than 8 hours without any separation anxiety symptoms.

Teaching him that separation has its rewards

He is conditioned to go into stress mode when he realizes you are leaving him. Right before you leave offer him a treat and you will be surprise that he might even begin to look forward for your departure. In this way you associate your departure with something positive. Additionally you can leave Kongs stuffed with any kind of treats, ready for him to dig into as soon as you leave. Lastly you can hide treats around the rooms so that he has something to do while you are gone.

Stay calm

When you are ready to leave from home, don't pay attention to him and leave those guilty and nervous feelings behind. If you are anxious or emotional about leaving might unintentionally transmit that tension to your puppy.

CHAPTER 6: TRAINING AND BASIC COMMANDS

You can start training at any age however the sooner the better. You can start simple training with your puppy as soon as he has settled into his new home. Older dogs are also receptive to training, although some may be less keen or less quick to learn than a younger dog. Done properly, training will be fun, both for you and your dog, as well as exercising his brain and reinforcing the good relationship between you.

Positive rewards

In order to be effective and to gain the best results, training should be based on positive rewards. Positive reward training works because if you reward your dog with something he wants as soon as he does what you ask, he is far more likely to do it again. Rewards can be anything that your puppy really wants and could include; food treats, a favorite toy, playing a certain game or getting a pat. However, really tasty treats will usually work best. Try small pieces of dried liver, hot dog sausage, chicken or cheese for maximum effect. If you are using food treats, you will need to reduce the size of your dog's normal meals or use his whole meal divided up into smaller portions, to prevent your dog putting on weight. Always combine the giving of a reward with verbal praise such as "Good dog".

When teaching a new command, you will need to reward your dog every time that he does what you ask correctly. Once your puppy 'gets it', it's a good idea to change the way you reward by only giving the reward every now and then. Always verbally praise your dog each time you exercise a command, even if he is not being rewarded with a treat.

THE EFFECTS OF PUNISHMENT AND REWARDS IN TRAINING

Punishment can cause distrust, fear, injury and aggression. Rubbing a dog nose in "it" can cause him to avoid going to the bathroom in front of you, electric fences can cause him to avoid his yard, and choke collars can cause throat injury and back and neck misalignment.

Punishments tend to escalate

If you were to resort to physical punishment, you would find that a light tap would get your dog's attention at first, but then the physical contact would tend to get more and more force behind it.

Punishment inhibits creativity

If your dog is punished for lying down when asked to sit, he will be confused and fearful.

Punishment has side effects

If his pinch collar tightens every time he sees another dog, he may not understand that it is his pulling that causes the pinch and may conclude that the other dog is the reason for his distress. Pinch or prong collars have been known to cause aggression towards other dogs.

We know better now

In the past, we punished children more harshly and have since learned better ways to motivate them. It is the same with our puppy.

Punishment can ruin your relationship with your puppy.

The act and mindset of looking for errors in your dog's behavior automatically place you in an adversarial relationship.

Training with punishment takes a lot of skill

Most people don't have this amount of skill. If you have poor timing or use too much force you can really harm your pet physically and psychologically. With reward training, the worst you can do is to be set back a bit or move more slowly until you become more skilled.

Punishment causes your puppy to focus on avoiding the punishment instead of changing the behavior

A traffic violator doesn't usually stop speeding. He just gets a radar detector. Your puppy will become adept at being a sneak or doing the minimum of a behavior to avoid punishment.

Your dog (and you) will not find training a pleasurable experience

There will be a lot of jerking and forcing going on and your dog will not want to participate.

Important Training tips- 'do's and 'don't's

Do:

• Practice in your home and garden first, before trying commands in public areas

• Start training with your new puppy as soon as possible

• Keep sessions short and fun (10 minutes max.)

• Train your puppy when he is hungry. Before his dinner time he will try harder for his treats

• Offer a reward or treat on a random basis, once the new command has been learnt.

• Try to use hand signals with verbal commands, as some dogs may find it easier to recognize

• Keep commands clear and consistent

• Be patient and take your time

• Stick to one command per training session at first to avoid confusing your dog

• Try to finish on a high note. Your dog is more likely to want to train again next time!

Don't:

• Let your dog get bored. Stop immediately if you see this happening

• Tell him off if he gets it wrong

• Shout or physically punish him. It will make him scared of you and may cause him to become aggressive.

• Train him if he is tired

• Chase him when you want him to come. He'll think it is a great game and will run away even more.

• Train him in an area with lots of distractions, such as other dogs, people, noises, smells.

• Expect too much too soon

THE BASIC COMMANDS

There are certain basic commands every dog should know. The basic commands that are useful for your dog to know are:

• *how to teach your Puppy his name*

• *sit,*

- *down,*
- *stay,*
- *come,*
- *heel*
- *leave it*

How to teach your Puppy his name

Teaching your puppy his name is a great way to start the training.

Step 1: To start with, armed with tasty treats and take your puppy somewhere with less destructions such as your house or your back yard.

Step 2: Put your dog on a long leash. By having a long leash, will help you to keep him from wandering off in case something attracts his attention.

Step 3: Have a treat in your hand. Wait until your puppy looks at you. Then say his name, give him the treat and praise with something like 'good dog'. It's very important that you say his name in a happy tone of voice. Then play with him briefly and repeat the exercise. By rewarding him with treats, praising him or playing with his favorite toy, you reinforce the desired behavior. Make sure to say his name only once for each exercise. The exercise becomes less effective if you repeat his name. In case that he does not respond, just gently tug his leash so he turns to look at you.

Step 4: Have a treat in your hand and hold it up near your face so that when you call his name, your puppy look directly at you. Then, give him the treat and praise. Doing this exercise will ensure that you have his full attention.

Step 5: Once your puppy response positively recognizing his name start practicing in areas with more distractions like the local park. You can also ask your friends to help by standing near the puppy and when the dog is not looking then have your friend to call his name and offer a treat.

With consistent patience and training, your puppy will eventually understand his own name.

Sit

This is the most basic command which helps you to keep control of your dog no matter the situation, and it is the best to start from. Show him that you have a food treat in your hand. Slowly move your hand and treat above and over his head towards his tail, as you give the command "sit". His head should go up as he tries to reach the treat, and his bottom should go down into the 'sit' position. Give him the treat and praise him. Do not push his bottom down to make him sit, as he is likely to push up against your hand and this may hurt his back.

When training your dog to sit, use the command "sit". Do not use "sit down" as this may confuse your dog when you try to teach the 'down' command.

Down

This is another useful command to train your puppy. Ask your dog to sit and show him the treat in your hand. Slowly move your hand down towards the ground in front of him (just in front of his feet), as you use the command "down". He should follow your hand with his nose and lay down. Give him the treat and praise him. If you have trouble getting him to lie down in this way, put an object such as a coffee table or a chair between you and your dog and try again. He will have to lie down to get under the barrier to get the treat. Remove the barrier when he gets the hang of it.

Do not push or force his back down as he will push against you and this may hurt his back.

Stay

Why teach stay? This is an excellent self-control exercise as well as having many practical uses, such as keeping your dog from bolting out of the door, jumping on people, and just keeping him still while you wait for your vet appointment. Do this exercise after teaching "Sit" and "Down" commands. To perfectly teach your puppy to stay, find a quiet place to practice and get your treats ready.

Turn your body to face him about a foot away, and hold your hand flat open up to his face and say 'Stay'. Now take one or two steps back. (If your dog gets up, this means you are proceeding too quickly.) Go back to where you were and use a "release word." (This may be something like "OK!"). Then praise and offer a reward.

Repeat this exercise and take several steps away until you can go out of sight. Work until you can have him stay for 2 minutes while you are in sight. (If you are very ambitious you can work on combining the 2 situations that is the stay and down).

In case that he has gotten up before you released him stay quiet and calmly return to where you were and get him back into 'sit' position using the hand signal as mentioned above.

Come

To get the puppy to effectively learn the 'Come' command, then find a quiet place to practice. Put a towel on the floor. Put a treat in your hand and use it to lure him to the towel as you say "come". If he starts moving toward you, give him verbal praise (This may be something like "Good boy!" and use a happy, encouraging tone of voice). Praise and offer a reward when all four feet are on the towel. Practice this about 10 times. Begin the exercise in the same way as above, hold your hand out as if you have a treat in it, but it will be empty (we will fool him a bit!). Repeat 10 times. Continue practicing using the empty-hand. Gradually turn this into an index-finger pointing hand-signal. Practice cueing come and pointing to the towel without walking all of the way to it with him. In case that your puppy doesn't come to you, then go slowly towards him and attach his leash. Then guide him back to the place where you called him to 'come'. You need to praise him the entire time to show him that you're not angry with him.

Heel

1st method: 'Heel[1]' means that your puppy is walking on your left side, while you hold the leash loosely. It's better to practice indoor or in

---

1.   http://www.akc.org/learn/akc-training/heeling-teach-dog-walk/

your garden first as there are fewer distractions for your dog than in the street.

Start with your puppy in the heel position (standing next to you). Hold his leash in your left hand and a treat in your right hand. Your right arm should be across the front of your body so the treat is above and slightly in front of your dog's head. Give the command 'heel' and step forward with confidence. Naturally your puppy should step forward. If the puppy moves to your side then praise and keep holding the treat in frond his head. In case your puppy gets distracted then squeaks the treat to get his attention and praise him if he looks up to you. After your puppy walks next to you for around 20 seconds give him the treat, praise and play with him for a while. Gradually increase the time he walks next to you. Once he gets used to executing this command means you can try this exercise outdoors.

2nd method: Alternatively, you can exercise heel command as above but this time without holding a treat. Give the command to your puppy to "heel". If he pulls, stand still immediately so that he has to stop, but do not say anything to him. Patiently wait until he comes back to your side and say "heel", praise and then step forward. If he continues to walk at your side, reinforce this behavior by using the command "heel" again. Then praise and offer him a treat. Every time that he pulls, you must stop. Your dog will soon learn that it is pointless to pull, as it will not get him anywhere and so should soon start to walk on your side.

It is a natural, enjoyable behavior for your puppy sniffing the ground, and fences for scents left by other dogs. On walks you should allow him to sniff around, but only when you say so and not when he feels like it. When he has been performing well use a command such as "off you go" so that he can learn when he is allowed to sniff. He's more likely to walk nicely because he knows that you will let him go sniff or go pee to an area he finds interesting.

Leave it

The "leave it" command allows you to tell your dog to leave or ignore an object that you don't want him to have, like eating food from the street (that might be harmful to him), or chew your child's toy, or anything he may try to pick up and chew.

Firstly hold a treat in your hand and allow your puppy to see and smell it. The moment he gets interested close your hand and say the command 'leave it'.

Usually most puppies will stick their nose on your hand or nibble on your fingers in an attempt to get the treat. Sooner or later your puppy will stop trying and pull away. This is the moment you need to praise and give him the treat. Make sure the treat that you give, is different than the one you told him to leave it. In the beginning stages of this command it is very important that you keep the treat covered so that the puppy cannot see it.

Once your puppy understands the concept of 'leave it' command you can make things little bit more difficult. Increase the time you make him wait for his treat. As soon as he pulls back you should offer the treat to the puppy and slowly add some seconds each time. You repeat this process until your puppy waits patiently for the treat for longer period of time. (some minutes).

Next you begin to step away. First place the treat on the floor and step back few steps. Naturally your puppy will proceed to 'investigate' the treat. When the puppy makes a lunge towards the treat then this is the moment that you will use the 'leave it' command. Make sure that you cover the treat so that your puppy cannot reach it, and do the exercise again. Slowly increase your distance from the treat. Keep training sessions short till your puppy has mastered the command.

CHAPTER 7: ACCEPTING HANDLING

This exercise will teach your dog to remain still and wait for a reward when you need to handle him for grooming or medical reasons and also to accept accidental inappropriate handling. It is an extremely important for your dog to learn to keep calm in order to prevent aggression.

Tips:

• Do not use your clicker (if you are using one) too close to his head! -It's okay to use a word such as "yes" or "good" and then deliver your treat, if clicking is awkward.

• Once your puppy has learned the following exercises with you, practice with other people.

• Easy cheese or peanut butter spread on the floor or refrigerator door is a simple way to keep your wiggly dog still for handling when you have not trained him yet to be still.

• If your puppy already dislikes being handled, you can teach him to accept it by following this method and going very slowly. Have a professional (or at least – someone else) do any needed manipulations such as grooming until he has learned to be comfortable. Muzzles do not hurt the puppy and can be helpful in keeping people safe while we teach him that it's okay to be handled.

• All dogs need to practice handling exercises for one or two minutes several times a week to remain calm.

For all the exercises, begin with very brief, non-invasive touches. If he stays still and calm and does not try to wiggle away continue touching him but do not resist his movement. Think of your hands as "sticky" - they will stay stuck to the dog but move with him until he is still and then offer a treat and release him.

Do not proceed to the next step until your dog enjoys the current one. Only work these exercises for a couple of minutes at a time.

Teaching your dog to accept handling of different body areas:

1. Collar: Find a quiet place to practice:

• Touch your dog's collar under his chin and immediately release him while you treat.

Repeat 10 times or until your puppy is happy about this exercise.

• Hold onto his collar under his chin for 2 seconds. Repeat until he is happy with this exercise. Increase the time gradually to 10 seconds.

• Hold his collar under his chin and tug on it a bit. If he wiggles, gently stay "stuck" to him until he calms and then release. Repeat this until he's comfortable and then try it from the top-side of his collar. Increase the intensity and duration slowly as you practice.

2. Paws: Many dogs are very sensitive about their paws. It is important to proceed slowly with this exercise so that your dog is enjoying it and to continue handling his paws throughout his lifetime. Do not trim your dog's nails unless you are absolutely sure you know what you are doing as it is easy to make a mistake and cause pain. Each step in this exercise should take several days to complete with dozens of repetitions. Complete each step before proceeding to the next one. Practice with all 4 paws.

• Pick up his paw and immediately treat him. Repeat 5 times and then progress to holding his paw for 1 second.

• Hold the paw for 10 seconds with no resistance from your dog.

• Hold the paw and move it around.

• Massage the paw.

• Pretend to trim the nails.

3. Ears:

• Reach around the side of your dog's head and touch his ear. Repeat 10 times.

• Once your puppy is comfortable, practice holding the ear for 1 second. If he wiggles, stay "stuck" to the ear, but move with him. If he stays still, treat him before releasing. Continue to practice this way until you can hold each ear for 10 seconds.

• Practice manipulating the ear and pretending to clean it. Remember to go slowly enough so that your dog enjoys it. It should take several days of practice before your dog will remain still for the "cleaning". If your dog is already sensitive about his ears, it may take longer.

4. Mouth:
- Gently touch your dog's mouth. Repeat 10 times.
- Touch the side of his mouth and pull up a lip to expose a tooth and release only when he is not resisting.
- Proceed slowly through the following steps: lifting the lip to expose more teeth, on both sides of the mouth and then try to open his mouth.
- Touch a tooth with a toothbrush and then work up to brushing his teeth for 1-10 seconds.

5. Tail: Many dogs are sensitive about having their tails handled.
- Begin by briefly touching your dog's tail. Repeat 10 times with treats. Once he's comfortable, proceed to being able to hold his tail for up to 10 seconds and then slowly pull the tail up and brush.

6. Touching by children:
- Prepare your dog with the strange sorts of touches given by children (always supervise and keep everyone safe when dogs and kids are together!) Practice by teaching him for accepting odd touches from you such as ear tugs, tail tugs, head pats, and hugs. As with all exercises proceed slowly.

7. Lifting:
- In an emergency, you may have to lift up even a large dog. Practice doing this by first putting your arms around him using treats for the briefest of touches and then proceed to being able to lift him off the ground while he remains calm. For dogs that require professional grooming, practice picking him up and putting him on a table.

8. Brushing:
- Get your dog's brush and lightly touch him with the brush. Repeat until he is comfortable while brushing him.

CHAPTER 8: POTTY TRAINING

Potty training is one of the most common challenges that pet owners face when they first adopt a new puppy. Puppies are fairly particular about where they "go" and build strong habits. It is very important to prevent accidents, because every time he relieves himself in the house, he is building a preference for that area. Keep in mind that your puppy can generally "hold it" for its age in months plus 1 hour.

Step 1

Until your dog has learned where to go potty, he should be under constant surveillance. In case that you cannot watch him continuously, you must put him back into his crate or pen in order to prevent "mistakes". The crate should be just big enough for him to stand up, turn around and lay down in. If your puppy is having accidents in the crate, make sure it isn't too big and remove absorbent bedding. Watch him constantly for sniffing or circling. Take him out immediately when you see this behavior.

Step 2

Set a timer to take your puppy out every hour (this time can be increased as you progress) so that you don't forget to take him out before nature calls. The more occasions you have that you can reward the appropriate behavior, the faster your puppy will learn to go potty. If he doesn't relieve himself when you take him out and it's been a few hours, take him back in for 15 minutes (under your closest supervision or crated) and then try bringing him back out again.

Step 3

In case you live in a flat or home with difficult outdoor access, use a bathroom or pen in your home for housetraining your puppy. Until he is reliably housetrained, bring him to the same spot each time, and leave a bit of his waste there. Use this spot only as a potty area, and not for play. Bring him there on leash and say something like "hurry up" when you see him getting ready. As he goes, say nothing so as not to distract him, but when he finishes praise, give him a tasty treat and spend 5 minutes playing outside away from the potty area. If he doesn't go, return to the house, put him in his crate and wait 15 minutes before trying again.

"But, what if he goes in the house..."

If you see your dog relieving itself in the wrong spot, bring him quickly to the potty area, and praise him for finishing there. If you find a mess, clean it very well (without him watching you) using a cleaner specific for pet stains. Be patient and avoid punishment in case of 'accidents'. Punishing your dog after an accident will not teach him anything, except that you are to be feared. Instead, try to take your puppy out more frequently.

Step 4

"How can I teach him to tell me when he needs to go out?"

Hang a bell near the door you use to take him out. Smear a bit of peanut butter on the bell and when he touches it and it rings, instantly open the door. Repeat each time you take him out to potty and eventually he will begin to ring it without the peanut butter. Now he will be able to tell you when he needs to go outside. (or when he just WANTS to go outside...to prevent this from happening, each time he rings the bell take him out for a potty break only. If he begins to play bring him back inside).

Lastly, in my experience, small dogs often take longer to potty train. My solution to the problem is to take them out more frequently than you would a large dog. Maximum time without a potty break as an adult should only equal about 4 hours. Many small dogs do very well with a litter box. I prefer this method because this way we can be sure that he can go whenever nature calls, even when it's a blizzard outside and he doesn't want to get his toes cold.

Even though most puppies are trained to relieve themselves outside , in some cases it make sense to teach your puppy to potty indoors in a specific area by using puppy pads, newspapers, litter or turf box. This training method is usually used by people who work long hours or people with health problems who cannot get outside easily. Pee puppy pads can also help sick and recuperating dogs or even fearful puppies[2] who haven't overcome their fears to relieve themselves outdoors. In such cases place the puppy pads in the same designated area and train your puppy to eliminate to that spot.

2.   http://dogtrainer.quickanddirtytips.com/how-to-help-your-shy-or-nervous-dog.aspx

CHAPTER 9: HOW TO GET YOUR PUPPY TO STOP BARKING

Dogs bark for many reasons. The most common are listed below with some ideas for solving the problem.

He wants attention:

He may want you to play or get up and feed him. Whatever it is... Don't do it! If you do, you will be teaching him that barking "works" to get his owner moving. Say "leave it" and then ignore him (don't even look at him – walk away or go into another room and close the door) until he stops for a few seconds and relaxes. Then you may do what he would like you to do. For the long term, make an effort to initiate activities he enjoys and make them happen on your schedule. Make sure that everything he gets he "earns". Have him "sit" to be given a privilege such as going outside, or getting his leash put on, his food bowl, petting, etc.

He is baking because he hears or sees something interesting:

When you are home:

1. Prevent: Block the source of sound/sights using a fan or blinds or keeping him in a different area of the house.

2. Teach "Quiet":

When your dog barks, wag a piece of food in front of his nose as you say "Quiet". When he stops barking then give the treat. After about 3 trials this way, the next time he barks, just "pretend" to be holding out a treat as you say "Quiet".

Reward him for choosing to be quiet on his own when he hears or sees something that usually makes him bark.

If he is unable to respond to the "Quiet" cue (or doesn't know it yet) just turn around and calmly walk away from the thing that is getting him so excited. Reward him when he becomes calm.

3. Use a "Time Out":

A "Time Out" (TO) should be used infrequently. By removing the dog from his social circle, you are administering what is called a negative punishment. This punishment can have side-effects that we don't necessarily want him learning that you walking towards him is a bad thing. This is why the TO should be used sparingly and an emphasis should be put on teaching the dog an alternative behavior that you prefer and preventing the misbehavior.

First, decide on a spot to use as a TO. The best spot is one that your dog finds boring - neither scary nor wonderful and is safe for him. Good examples are a gated pantry, bathroom (remove the toilet paper first!) or tether. If your dog does not mind his crate, you can use that as a TO area. Have him wear a 2-foot piece of rope with a knot on the end. When your dog barks, say "time out" in a neutral voice, walk calmly to him, grasp the rope and walk him gently but firmly to his time out space. Place him there for 5 minutes (or longer if you need a time out from him!). After the 5 minutes, if he is calm, release him. He may need you to demonstrate this a few times before he understands which behavior is earning him the TO.

4. Use a Citronella Spray Collar:

This should be reserved for when you "can't take it anymore!" and the barking is not associated with fear or aggression. You will have to first use the collar when you are home to make sure he understands how it works.

On a walk (barking at other dogs, people. or cars, etc out of excitement):

1. Teach him "Watch Me":

Begin in the house with few distractions present. Say your dog's name and "Watch me" while holding a treat to your nose. When your dog looks at the treat wait for 1 second and give it. Practice this 10 times. Then practice it while only "pretending" to have a treat. This will become your hand signal. Build up the length of time that your dog can continue watching you.

Practice "watch me" while you are walking around inside or while you are outside (you may need to revert to showing him the treat for a few reps) or even when you are outside near something interesting. In general, practice "watch me" in a situation when he would normally bark.

2. Teach "Quiet":

Teach him the "Quiet" cue as explained above.

When he begins to bark or you see one of his triggers, say "Quiet". Teach him that his trigger means "Quiet". Example: barking at cars.

Whenever a car goes by waggle a treat in his face and bring it towards yours. When he looks at you offer him a reward. Repeat until he voluntarily looks at you (without barking) when a car is coming.

If he is unable to respond to the "Quiet" cue (or doesn't know it yet) just turn around and calmly walk away from the thing that is getting him so excited. Reward him when he becomes calm.

He is excited to play:

Teach him that when he begins to bark the play ends. Leave a short leash on him if you need to, in order to lead him out of the play session. When he begins to bark, teach him the 'time out' (see above) or stop playing with him. Offer a reward if only after he is quiet.

He is afraid, aggressive or territorial:

Prevent outbursts by crating, gating, blocking windows, using a fan or not taking him places that cause him to have outbursts. This is not meant to be a permanent solution but it's helpful while you are teaching him that he does not need to be afraid. It is best to do this for 7 days before the beginning of the training, to give his body and mind a chance to calm down.

When the trigger appears at a distance gradually get him closer to the trigger point. For a territorially aggressive dog, it may be helpful to teach him that the doorbell (or knock) means he should get in his crate and wait for treats. You can begin to teach this by ringing the doorbell and then luring him to his crate and feeding treats.

It's also helpful to lure him through his fears if possible. For instance, if you are on a walk and confront one of his triggers get his attention and put a treat to his nose to lead him along. Continue feeding him until you are out of the "danger zone".

Teach him "Watch Me" (see above). Use this method when you predict he will get nervous and offer him treats frequently for watching you. Make sure to reward calm behavior.

He is bored or frustrated:

Prevent by keeping him busy and tiring him out playing with chew toys, exercise or training. He should have at least 30 minutes of exercise per day, plus 1 hour of chewing and 15 minutes of training.

Teach "Quiet" (see above). Reward him for choosing to be quiet on his own when he hears or sees something that usually makes him bark. Lastly use a "Timeout" method (see above).

CHAPTER 10: HOW TO STOP MY PUPPY FROM BITING AND CHEWING THINGS

If your puppy is starting to bite your hands, chew furniture, shoes or something else, then you must find out ways to stop this behavior. When the puppy is below six months old, he will go through a period of teething in the same way as babies do. Teething can be a painful process for the puppy, so you need to understand that puppy biting will happen all the time during his period of aging. The puppy rubs his gums when chewing and that feels really nice to him. Puppy will chew your belongings because they have your distinct smell on them and that additionally comforts him. However, training your puppy not to chew things or mouthing you is easier than you think.

Step 1

First thing you need to do is to keep your things away from the puppy when you are not around him. When it comes to your furniture, you can cover the chewing areas of your furniture such as the shelf edges or sofa legs with some bad-tasting substance like pepper, or other various products, such as bitter apple, bitter cherry, that are designed to prevent a dog from licking or chewing. Buying some soft dog chew toys is also advisable, as the puppy will focus more on them instead on your furniture or on human skin. Avoid punishing your puppy. Do not be aggressive with your puppy and avoid playing aggressive games like wrestling or chasing. This is because if you do this you will encourage your puppy to start biting things with excitement and the puppy will learn to associate biting and nipping with fun activities. As soon as your puppy is trained that biting is not good behavior, then you can start playing physical games with him.

Step 2

Start playing with your puppy and let him mouth on your hands until he bites hard and give a high-pitched yelping sound as if you are hurt and let your hand go limp. This should stop your puppy from biting. If it seems that the yelp has no effect then you can use a loud, "Ow!

When your puppy stops mouthing, praise and offer him a treat. Then resume play. It's important to remember that you should not repeat the limp and yelp process more than three times in fifteen minutes and then you should go to step 3. Furthermore, encourage good behavior. Every time your little puppy behaves good and does not bite, make sure you tell him some good pleasant words and pet him on his head and body. This way you will encourage your little puppy to stop mouthing and biting.

Step 3

If step 2 doesn't work you can switch to Time – Out procedure which can be effective in such cases. In this exercise, you will teach him that gentle play continues, but painful play stops. Start playing with your dog and when he starts mouthing you again, remove your hand from his mouth and ignore for 20 seconds. If he keeps mouthing you then get up and move away to another room. Repeat this method until your puppy can play with your hands very gently and you don't feel any pressure from his teeth.

Step 4:

Another thing you can do is to remove your hand from his mouth before contact and replace it with some dog chew toys which will be soft enough for him to play with in order to satisfy your puppy's urge to mouth things. You can also distract him by giving him treats from your other hand. In this way you teach him getting used to being touched without mouthing.

Another way to help your puppy to understand that his mouth on human skin is not okay at all is to teach him to be obedient. You can also enroll him into a specialized training class where he will socialize with other puppies and will get a proper training about how to behave in a positive way. Important thing to have in mind is that your puppy cannot learn everything overnight so be patient and know that this is a slow process.

By following these easy steps you can rest assured that your puppy will grow into a good and healthy dog.

CHAPTER 11: CONCLUSION

Try to have realistic expectations from your dog. They are, after all, animals, no matter what you do, you cannot expect them to do their job, and clean up the potty and walk around with a clean behind. Keep in mind that every time your puppy makes a mistake, he's giving you a perfect opportunity to train him and teach him what you expect of him.

Lastly, you are never done training your dog but I assure this will go a long way in helping you to get the perfect mutual relationship with your puppy.

CPSIA information can be obtained
at www.ICGtesting.com
Printed in the USA
BVHW070452220921
617192BV00011B/1399